The Collins Book of NURSERY RHYMES

BOOK CLUB ASSOCIATES
London

Illustrations

NIKI DALY   AMANDA DAVIDSON

SALLY HOLMES   JULIA HUTTON   CAROLYN PAVEY

IRIS SCHWEITZER   CAROLINE SHARPE

William Collins Sons & Co. Ltd
London · Glasgow · Sydney · Auckland
Toronto · Johannesburg

This edition published 1982 by
Book Club Associates
By arrangement with William Collins Sons & Co Ltd

ISBN 0 00 195215 3
First published 1981
Copyright © this collection, 1981
Origination by Culver Graphics Litho Ltd
Printed by William Collins Sons & Co. Ltd

This collection of traditional rhymes and songs
will delight small readers
and remind their parents of nursery days.

Lullabies and counting rhymes,
cherry stone games and cautionary tales, nonsense,
dips, skipping songs, hopscotch chants
and ring games – all the old favourites are
here to be enjoyed anew.

Contents

Let's begin

Out goes the rat,
Out goes the cat,
Out goes the lady   With the big green hat.
Y, O, U, spells you;
O, U, T, spells out!

Dip dip dip,
My blue ship,
Sailing on the water,
Like a cup and saucer.
Dip dip dip,
You're not It.

Eenie, meenie, minie, mo,
Catch a tiger by the toe,
If he hollers, let him go,
Eenie, meenie, minie, mo.

Ickle ockle, blue bockle,
    Fishes in the sea,
If you want a pretty maid,
    Please choose me.

One potato, two potato,
Three potato, four;
Five potato, six potato,
Seven potato, MORE.

11

A is for anchor to fasten the boat,
   B is for badger with black and white coat.
C is for cloud, high in the sky,
   D is for doll with boot-button eye.
E is for elephant. He's just done a trick,
   F is a flower you may want to pick.
G's a giraffe, with neck long and thin,
   H is a house; lift the latch and come in.
I is for inkwell with label and lid,
   J is for jelly, delicious and red.
K is a kite on the end of a string,
   L is for lion, proud as a king.
M is the moon that lightens the night,
   N is for nothing. There's nothing in sight.
O is an orange, juicy and sweet,
   P is a pie, ready to eat.
Q is for queen, with a crown on her head,
   R is for rainbow, coloured violet to red.
S is a star in the night sky a-glowing,
   T is a tree with green leaves a-blowing.
U's an umbrella that's blown right away,
   V's a volcano that burns night and day.
W's a whale. It lives in the sea,
   X an xylophone, to make music for me.
Y is for yellow, yellow like butter,
   Z is for zebra, and the last letter I'll utter.

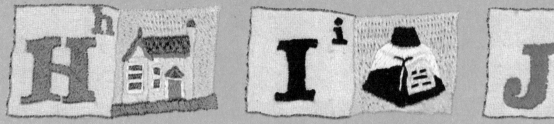

One to ten, and then again

One, two, three,
I love coffee,
And Billy loves tea,
How good you be,
One, two, three,
I love coffee,
And Billy loves tea.

One, two, three, four, five,
Once I caught a fish alive,
Six, seven, eight, nine, ten,
Then I let it go again.
Why did you let it go?
Because it bit my finger so.
Which finger did it bite?
The little finger on the right.

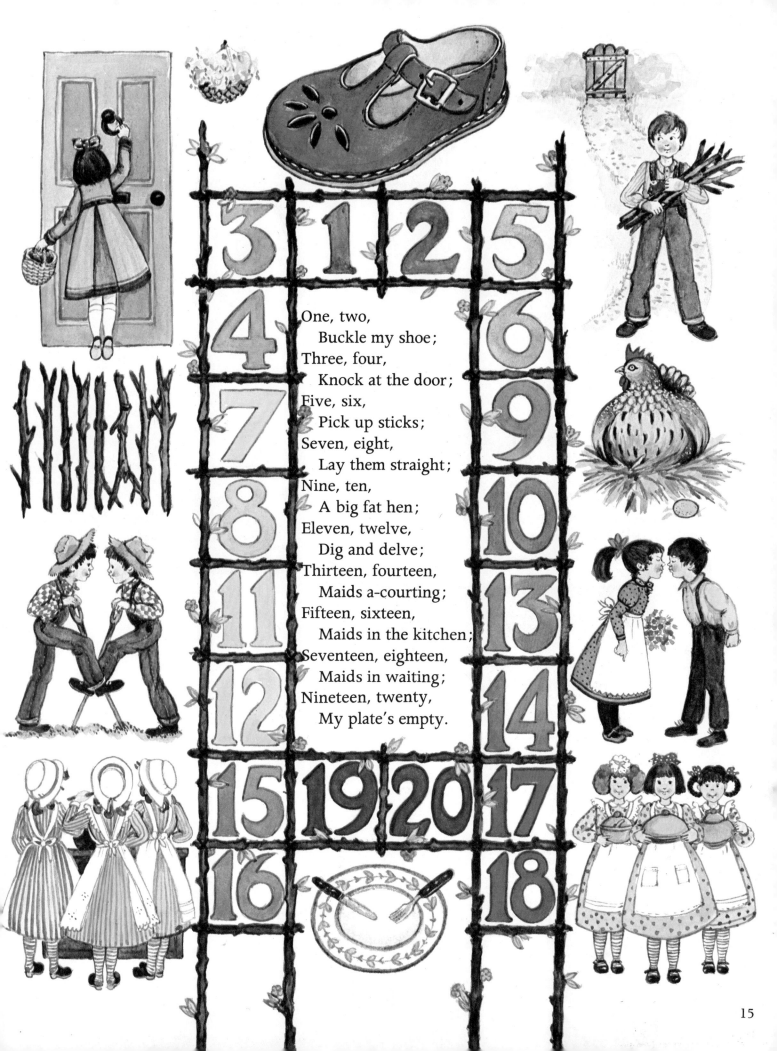

One, two,
  Buckle my shoe;
Three, four,
  Knock at the door;
Five, six,
  Pick up sticks;
Seven, eight,
  Lay them straight;
Nine, ten,
  A big fat hen;
Eleven, twelve,
  Dig and delve;
Thirteen, fourteen,
  Maids a-courting;
Fifteen, sixteen,
  Maids in the kitchen;
Seventeen, eighteen,
  Maids in waiting;
Nineteen, twenty,
  My plate's empty.

Nursery days

Bye, baby bunting,
Daddy's gone a-hunting,
Gone to get a rabbit skin
To wrap the baby bunting in.

Pat-a-cake, pat-a-cake, baker's man,
Bake me a cake as fast as you can;
Pat it and prick it, and mark it with B,
Put it in the oven for Baby and me.

Dance to your daddy,
   My little babby,
Dance to your daddy,
   My little lamb.

You shall have a fishy
   In a little dishy,
You shall have a fishy
   When the boat comes in.

You shall have an apple,
   You shall have a plum,
You shall have a rattle-basket
   When your daddy comes home.

Hush-a-bye, baby, on the tree top,
When the wind blows, the cradle will rock;
When the bough breaks, the cradle will fall,
And down will come baby, cradle and all.

How many days has my baby to play?
Saturday, Sunday, Monday,
Tuesday, Wednesday, Thursday, Friday,
Saturday, Sunday, Monday.
Hop away, skip away,
My baby wants to play;
My baby wants to play every day!

Baby games

This little piggy went to market;
This little piggy stayed at home;
This little piggy had roast beef;
This little piggy had none;
This little piggy cried, Wee, wee, wee,
All the way home.

Tickly, tickly, on your knee,
If you laugh you don't love me.

Round and round the garden,
Like a teddy bear;
One step, two step,
Tickle you under there!

This is the way the ladies ride,
  Nim, nim, nim, nim.
This is the way the gentlemen ride,
  Trim, trim, trim, trim.
This is the way the farmers ride,
  Trot, trot, trot, trot.
This is the way the huntsmen ride,
  A-gallop, a-gallop, a-gallop.
This is the way the ploughboys ride,
  Hobble-dy-hoy, hobble-dy-hoy.

Clap hands, Daddy comes
With his pocket full of plums,
  And a cake for *you*.

Here are the lady's knives and forks,
Here is the lady's table,
Here is the lady's looking-glass,
And here is the baby's cradle.

Three Little Kittens

Three little kittens
They lost their mittens,
   And they began to cry,
Oh, mother dear,
We sadly fear
   Our mittens we have lost.
What! lost your mittens,
You naughty kittens!
   Then you shall have no pie.
Mee-ow, mee-ow, mee-ow.
No, you shall have no pie.

The three little kittens
They found their mittens,
   And they began to cry,
Oh, mother dear,
See here, see here,
   Our mittens we have found.
Put on your mittens,
You silly kittens,
   And you shall have some pie.
Purr-r, purr-r, purr-r,
Oh, let us have some pie.

The three little kittens
Put on their mittens
    And soon ate up the pie;
Oh, mother dear,
We greatly fear
    Our mittens we have soiled.
What! soiled your mittens,
You naughty kittens!
    Then they began to sigh,
    Mee-ow, mee-ow, mee-ow,
    Then they began to sigh.

The three little kittens
They washed their mittens,
    And hung them out to dry;
Oh! mother dear,
Do you not hear,
    Our mittens we have washed.
What! washed your mittens,
Then you're good kittens,
    But I smell a rat close by.
    Mee-ow, mee-ow, mee-ow,
    We smell a rat close by.

I Love Little Pussy

I love little pussy,
  Her coat is so warm,
And if I don't hurt her
  She'll do me no harm.
So I'll not pull her tail,
  Nor drive her away,
But pussy and I
  Very gently will play.
She shall sit by my side,
  And I'll give her some food;
And pussy will love me
  Because I am good.

Pussy cat Mole jumped over a coal,
And in her best petticoat burned a
  great hole.
Poor pussy's weeping, she'll have
  no more milk,
Until her best petticoat's mended
  with silk.

Pussy cat ate the dumplings,
Pussy cat ate the dumplings,
  Mamma stood by,
  And cried, Oh, fie!
Why did you eat the dumplings?

Sing, sing,
  What shall I sing?
The cat's run away
  With the pudding string!
Do, do,
  What shall I do?
The cat's run away
  With the pudding too!

Ding, dong, bell,
Pussy's in the well.
Who put her in?
Little Johnny Green.
Who pulled her out?
Little Tommy Stout.
What a naughty boy was that
To try to drown poor pussy cat,
Who never did him any harm,
And killed the mice in his father's barn.

Who's that ringing at my door bell?
    A little pussy cat that isn't very well.
Rub its little nose with a little mutton fat,
    That's the best cure for a little pussy cat.

23

Mice galore

Three blind mice, see how they run!
They all ran after the farmer's wife,
Who cut off their tails with a carving knife,
Did you ever see such a thing in your life,
As three blind mice?

Three young rats with black felt hats,

Three young ducks with white straw flats,

Three young dogs with curling tails,

Three young cats with demi-veils,

Went out to walk with two young pigs
In satin vests and sorrel wigs;

But suddenly it chanced to rain
And so they all went home again.

Hickory, dickory, dock,
The mouse ran up the clock.
The clock struck one,
The mouse ran down,
Hickory, dickory, dock.

Six little mice sat down to spin;
Pussy passed by and she peeped in.
What are you doing, my little men?
Weaving coats for gentlemen.
Shall I come in and cut off your threads?
No, no, Mistress Pussy,
You'd bite off our heads.
Oh, no, I'll not; I'll help you to spin.
That may be so, but you don't come in.

Cock Robin

Who killed Cock Robin?
  I, said the Sparrow,
  With my bow and arrow,
I killed Cock Robin.

Who saw him die?
  I, said the Fly,
  With my little eye,
I saw him die.

Who caught his blood?
  I, said the Fish,
  With my little dish,
I caught his blood.

Who'll make his shroud?
  I, said the Beetle,
  With my thread and needle,
I'll make the shroud.

Who'll dig his grave?
  I, said the Owl,
  With my pick and shovel,
I'll dig his grave.

Who'll be the parson?
  I, said the Rook,
  With my little book,
I'll be the parson.

Who'll be the clerk?
  I, said the Lark,
  If it's not in the dark,
I'll be the clerk.

Who'll carry the link?
  I, said the Linnet,
  I'll fetch it in a minute,
I'll carry the link.

Who'll be chief mourner?
  I, said the Dove,
  I mourn for my love,
I'll be chief mourner.

Who'll carry the coffin?
  I, said the Kite,
  If it's not through the night,
I'll carry the coffin.

Who'll bear the pall?
  We, said the Wren,
  Both the cock and the hen,
We'll bear the pall.

Who'll sing a psalm?
  I, said the Thrush,
  As she sat on a bush,
I'll sing a psalm.

Who'll toll the bell?
  I, said the Bull,
  Because I can pull,
So Cock Robin, farewell.

All the birds of the air
  Fell a-sighing and a-sobbing,
When they heard the bell toll
  For poor Cock Robin.

27

Sing a Song of Sixpence

Sing a song of sixpence,
A pocket full of rye;
Four and twenty blackbirds,
Baked in a pie.

When the pie was opened,
The birds began to sing;
Wasn't that a dainty dish,
To set before the king?

The king was in his counting-house,
    Counting out his money;
The queen was in the parlour,
    Eating bread and honey.

The maid was in the garden,
    Hanging out the clothes,
When down came a blackbird
    And pecked off her nose.

Birds of the air

A wise old owl sat in an oak,
The more he heard the less he spoke;
The less he spoke the more he heard.
Why aren't we all like that wise old bird?

Jenny Wren fell sick
Upon a merry time,
In came Robin Redbreast
And brought her sops and wine.

Eat well of the sop, Jenny,
Drink well of the wine.
Thank you, Robin, kindly,
You shall be mine.

Jenny Wren got well,
And stood upon her feet;
And told Robin plainly,
She loved him not a bit.

Robin he got angry,
And hopped upon a twig,
Saying, Out upon you, fie upon you,
Bold faced jig!

Little Robin Redbreast
Came to visit me;
This is what he whistled,
Thank you for my tea.

Pit, pat, well-a-day,
Little Robin flew away.
Where can little Robin be?
Gone into the cherry tree.

Little Poll Parrot
Sat in his garret
Eating toast and tea;
   A little brown mouse
   Jumped into the house,
And stole it all away.

There were two birds sat on a stone,
   Fa, la, la, la, lal, de;
One flew away, and then there was one,
   Fa, la, la, la, lal, de;
The other flew after, and then there was none,
   Fa, la, la, la, lal, de;
And so the poor stone was left all alone,
   Fa, la, la, la, lal, de.

I Saw a Ship a-Sailing

I saw a ship a-sailing,
A-sailing on the sea,
And oh, but it was laden
With pretty things for thee!

There were comfits in the cabin,
And apples in the hold;
The sails were made of silk,
And the masts were all of gold.

The four-and-twenty sailors,
That stood between the decks,
Were four-and-twenty white mice
With chains about their necks.

The captain was a duck
With a packet on his back,
And when the ship began to move
The captain said, Quack! Quack!

Quack Quack

When I was young I used to go
With my daddy's dinner-o,
Baked potatoes, beef and steak,
Two red herrings, and a ha'penny cake;
I came to a river
And I couldn't get across,
I paid two pound
For an old dun horse,
Jumped on its back,
Its bones gave a crack;
I played upon my fiddle
Till the boat came back.

The House that Jack Built

This is the house that Jack built.

This is the malt
That lay in the house
that Jack built.

This is the rat,
That ate the malt
That lay in the house
that Jack built.

This is the cat,
That killed the rat,
That ate the malt
That lay in the house
that Jack built.

This is the dog,
That worried the cat,
That killed the rat,
That ate the malt
That lay in the house
that Jack built.

This is the cow with the crumpled horn,
That tossed the dog,
That worried the cat,
That killed the rat,
That ate the malt
That lay in the house
that Jack built.

This is the maiden all forlorn,
That milked the cow with the crumpled horn,
That tossed the dog,
That worried the cat,
That killed the rat,
That ate the malt
That lay in the house
that Jack built.

This is the man all tattered and torn,
That kissed the maiden all forlorn,
That milked the cow
with the crumpled horn,
That tossed the dog,
That worried the cat,
That killed the rat,
That ate the malt
That lay in the house
that Jack built.

This is the priest all shaven and shorn,
That married the man all tattered and torn,
That kissed the maiden all forlorn,
That milked the cow with the crumpled horn,
That tossed the dog,
That worried the cat,
That killed the rat,
That ate the malt
That lay in the house
that Jack built.

This is the cock that crowed in the morn,
That waked the priest all shaven and shorn,
That married the man all tattered and torn,
That kissed the maiden all forlorn,
That milked the cow with the crumpled horn,
That tossed the dog,
That worried the cat,
That killed the rat,
That ate the malt
That lay in the house
that Jack built.

Nonsensical rhymes

Hey diddle, diddle,
The cat and the fiddle,
The cow jumped over the moon;
The little dog laughed
To see such sport,
And the dish ran away with
the spoon.

Rub-a-dub-dub,
Three men in a tub,
And how do you think they got there?
The butcher, the baker,
The candlestick-maker,
They all jumped out of a rotten potato,
'Twas enough to make a man stare.

A man in the wilderness, he asked me,
How many strawberries grow in the sea.
I answered him, as I thought good,
As many red herrings as swim in the wood.

37

Humpty Dumpty sat on a wall,
Humpty Dumpty had a great fall;
All the King's horses
And all the King's men
Couldn't put Humpty together again.

Owen Moore went away,
Owing more than he could pay.
Owen Moore came back next day,
Owing more.

Hoddley, poddley, puddle and fogs,
Cats are to marry the poodle dogs;
Cats in blue jackets and dogs in red hats,
What will become of the mice and the rats?

Mother, may I go out to swim?
    Yes, my darling daughter.
Hang your clothes on a hickory limb
    And don't go near the water.

The Key
to the Kingdom

This is the key of the kingdom:
In that kingdom is a city,
In that city is a town,
In that town there is a street,
In that street there winds a lane,
In that lane there is a yard,
In that yard there is a house,
In that house there waits a room,
In that room there is a bed,
On that bed there is a basket,
   A basket of flowers.

Flowers in the basket,
Basket on the bed,
Bed in the chamber,
Chamber in the house,
House in the weedy yard,
Yard in the winding lane,
Lane in the broad street,
Street in the high town,
Town in the city,
City in the kingdom:
   This is the key of the kingdom.

In the city,
   in the street

Up and down the City Road,
   In and out the Eagle,
That's the way the money goes,
   Pop goes the weasel!

Half a pound of tuppenny rice,
   Half a pound of treacle,
Mix it up and make it nice,
   Pop goes the weasel!

Every night when I go out
   The monkey's on the table;
Take a stick and knock it off,
   Pop goes the weasel!

London Bridge is falling down,
Falling down, falling down;
London Bridge is falling down,
My fair lady.

We must build it up again,
Up again, up again;
We must build it up again,
My fair lady.

Oranges and lemons,
    Say the bells of St Clement's.
You owe me five farthings,
    Say the bells of St Martin's.
When will you pay me?
    Say the bells of Old Bailey.
When I grow rich,
    Say the bells of Shoreditch.
When will that be?
    Say the bells of Stepney.
I'm sure I don't know,
    Says the Great Bell of Bow.

Sally go round the sun,
Sally go round the moon,
Sally go round the chimney-pots
On a Saturday afternoon.

Mary had a Little Lamb

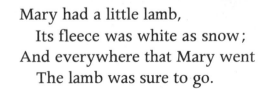

Mary had a little lamb,
    Its fleece was white as snow;
And everywhere that Mary went
    The lamb was sure to go.

It followed her to school one day,
    That was against the rule;
It made the children laugh and play
    To see a lamb at school.

And so the teacher turned it out,
But still it lingered near,
And waited patiently about
Till Mary did appear.

Why does the lamb love Mary so?
The eager children cry;
Why, Mary loves the lamb, you know,
The teacher did reply.

Down on the farm

Come, butter, come,
Come, butter, come,
Peter stands at the gate
Waiting for a butter cake.
Come, butter, come.

If I had a donkey that wouldn't go,
Would I beat him? Oh no, no.
I'd put him in the barn and give him some corn,
The best little donkey that ever was born.

Little Bo-peep has lost her sheep,
   And doesn't know where to find them;
Leave them alone, and they'll come home,
   Bringing their tails behind them.

Baa, baa, black sheep,
   Have you any wool?
Yes, sir, yes, sir,
   Three bags full;
One for the master,
   And one for the dame,
And one for the little boy
   Who lives down the lane.

Going for a ride!

Shoe a little horse,
Shoe a little mare,
But let the little colt
Go bare, bare, bare.

Yankee Doodle came to town,
    Riding on a pony;
He stuck a feather in his cap
    And called it macaroni.

I had a little pony,
    His name was Dapple Gray;
I lent him to a lady
    To ride a mile away.
She whipped him, she slashed him,
    She rode him through the mire;
I would not lend my pony now,
    For all the lady's hire.

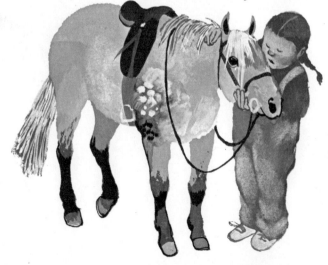

Ride a cock-horse to Banbury Cross,
To see a fine lady upon a white horse;
Rings on her fingers and bells on her toes,
She shall have music wherever she goes.

48

A farmer went trotting upon his grey mare,
    Bumpety, bumpety, bump!
With his daughter behind him so rosy and fair,
    Lumpety, lumpety, lump!

A raven cried, Croak! and they all tumbled down,
    Bumpety, bumpety, bump!
The mare broke her knees and the farmer his crown,
    Lumpety, lumpety, lump!

The mischievous raven flew laughing away,
    Bumpety, bumpety, bump!
And vowed he would serve them the same the next day,
    Lumpety, lumpety, lump!

Cherry stone rhymes

Who shall I marry?

Tinker,
Tailor,
Soldier,
Sailor,
Rich man,
Poor man,
Beggar man,
Thief.

When will it be?

This year,
Next year,
Sometime,
Never.

Where shall I marry?

Church,
Chapel,
Cathedral,
Abbey.

And the ring?

Gold,
Silver,
Copper,
Brass.

How shall I get there?

Coach,
Carriage,
Wheelbarrow,
Dustcart.

What shall I wear?

Silk,
Satin,
Cotton,
Rags.

And where shall we live happily ever after?

Big house,
Little house,
Pig sty,
Barn.

What's for dinner?

Davy Davy Dumpling,
　Boil him in the pot;
Sugar him and butter him,
　And eat him while he's hot.

Polly put the kettle on,
Polly put the kettle on,
Polly put the kettle on,
　We'll all have tea.

Sukey take it off again,
Sukey take it off again,
Sukey take it off again,
　They've all gone away.

Pease porridge hot,
Pease porridge cold,
Pease porridge in the pot
Nine days old.
Some like it hot,
Some like it cold,
Some like it in the pot
Nine days old.

NINE
DAYS
OLD

Little Miss Muffet
Sat on a tuffet,
Eating her curds and whey;
There came a big spider,
Who sat down beside her
And frightened Miss Muffet away.

Little Tommy Tucker
    Sings for his supper:
What shall we give him?
    White bread and butter.
How shall he cut it
    Without e'er a knife?
How will he be married
    Without e'er a wife?

Jack Sprat could eat no fat,
    His wife could eat no lean,
And so between them both, you see,
    They licked the platter clean.

Bad boys and naughty girls

Little Tommy Tittlemouse
Lived in a little house;
He caught fishes
In other men's ditches.

There was a little girl, and she had a little curl
Right in the middle of her forehead;
When she was good she was very, very good,
But when she was bad she was horrid.

Elsie Marley is grown so fine,
She won't get up to feed the swine,
But lies in bed till eight or nine.
Lazy Elsie Marley.

Georgie Porgie, pudding and pie,
Kissed the girls and made them cry;
When the boys came out to play,
Georgie Porgie ran away.

Handy Pandy Jack-a-Dandy
Stole a piece of sugar candy
From the grocer's shoppy-shop,
And away did hoppy-hop.

Diddle, diddle, dumpling, my son John,
Went to bed with his trousers on;
One shoe off, and one shoe on,
Diddle, diddle, dumpling, my son John.

Little Polly Flinders
Sat among the cinders,
Warming her pretty little toes;
Her mother came and caught her,
And whipped her little daughter
For spoiling her nice new clothes.

Jack and Jill

Jack and Jill
Went up the hill,
To fetch a pail of water;
Jack fell down,
And broke his crown,
And Jill came tumbling after.

Then up Jack got,
And home did trot,
As fast as he could caper;
He went to bed,
To mend his head,
With vinegar and brown paper.

Off to the shop!

Little girl, little girl,
    Where have you been?
I've been to see grandmother
    Over the green.
What did she give you?
    Milk in a can.
What did you say for it?
    Thank you, Grandam.

I went into my grandmother's garden,
And there I found a farthing.
I went into my next door neighbour's;
There I bought
A pipkin and a popkin,
A slipkin and a slopkin,
A nailboard, a sailboard,
And all for a farthing.

Who comes here?
  A grenadier.
What do you want?
  A pot of beer.
Where's your money?
  I forgot it.
Get you gone,
  You silly blockhead.

Buttons, a farthing a pair,
  Come, who will buy them of me?
They are round and sound and pretty
And fit for the girls of the city.
  Come, who will buy them of me?
  Buttons, a farthing a pair.

To market, to market,
  To buy a plum bun;
Home again, home again,
  Market is done.

Trit trot to market
To buy a penny doll,
Trit trot back again,
The market's sold them all

Billy and Betty

When shall we be married,
　Billy, my own sweet lad?
We shall be married tomorrow,
　If you think it is good.
Shall we be married no sooner,
　Billy, my own sweet lad?
Would you be married tonight?
　I think that the girl is gone mad.

Who shall we ask to the wedding,
　Billy, my own sweet lad?
We shall ask father and mother,
　If you think it is good.
Shall we ask nobody else,
　Billy, my own sweet lad?
Would you ask King and Queen?
　I think that the girl is gone mad.

What shall I wear to the wedding,
    Billy, my own sweet lad?
You have your apron and gown,
    If you think it is good.
Shall I wear nothing that's finer,
    Billy, my own sweet lad?
Would you wear satin and silk?
    I think that the girl is gone mad.

What shall we have for the dinner,
    Billy, my own sweet lad?
We shall have bacon and beans,
    If you think it is good.
Shall we have nothing more,
    Billy, my own sweet lad?
Would you have peaches and cream?
    I think that the girl is gone mad.

How shall I go to the church,
    Billy, my own sweet lad?
You shall ride in my wheelbarrow,
    If you think it is good.
Shall I have nothing that's better,
    Billy, my own sweet lad?
Would you have horses and coach?
    I think that the girl is gone mad.

Pigs to market

To market, to market, to buy a fat pig,
Home again, home again, jiggety jig;
To market, to market, to buy a fat hog,
Home again, home again, jiggety jog.

FOR SALE

SOLD

Dickery, dickery, dare,
The pig flew up in the air;
The man in brown
Soon brought him down,
Dickery, dickery, dare.

Tom, Tom, the piper's son,
Stole a pig and away he run;
The pig was eat,
And Tom was beat,
And Tom went howling down the street.

Higglety, pigglety, pop!
The dog has eaten the mop;
The pig's in a hurry,
The cat's in a flurry,
Higglety, pigglety, pop!

Whose Little Pigs?

Whose little pigs are these, these, these?
  Whose little pigs are these?
They are Roger the Cook's, I know by their looks;
  I found them among my peas.
Go pound them, go pound them.
  I dare not on my life,
For though I love not Roger the Cook,
  I dearly love his wife.

Rain, rain, go away!

Blow, wind, blow!
And go, mill, go!
That the miller may grind his corn;
That the baker may take it,
And into bread make it,
And bring us a loaf in the morn.

Rain on the green grass,
And rain on the tree,
Rain on the house-top,
But not on me.

March winds and April showers
Bring forth May flowers.

Ipsey Wipsey spider
    Climbing up the spout;
Down came the rain
    And washed the spider out:
Out came the sunshine
    And dried up all the rain;
Ipsey Wipsey spider
    Climbing up again.

A sunshiny shower
Won't last half an hour.

Rain, rain, go away,
Come again another day,
Little Johnny wants to play.

Lazy days

Ladybird, ladybird,
  Fly away home,
Your house is on fire
  And your children are gone;
All except one
  And that's little Ann
And she has crept under
  The frying pan.

A diller, a dollar,
A ten o'clock scholar,
What makes you come so soon?
You used to come at ten o'clock,
But now you come at noon.

Buttercups and daisies,
  Oh what pretty flowers,
Coming in the springtime
  To tell of sunny hours.
While the trees are leafless,
  While the fields are bare,
Buttercups and daisies
  Spring up everywhere.

The cock's on the wood pile
  Blowing his horn,
The bull's in the barn
  A-threshing the corn,
The maids in the meadow
  Are making the hay,
The ducks in the river
  Are swimming away.

A swarm of bees in May
Is worth a load of hay;
A swarm of bees in June
Is worth a silver spoon;
A swarm of bees in July
Is not worth a fly.

Little Boy Blue,
  Come blow your horn,
The sheep's in the meadow,
  The cow's in the corn.
Where is the boy
  Who looks after the sheep?
He's under a haycock
  Fast asleep.
Will you wake him?
  No, not I,
For if I do,
  He's sure to cry.

The Fox's Foray

A fox jumped up one winter's night,
And begged the moon to give him light,
For he'd many miles to trot that night
Before he reached his den O!
    Den O! Den O!
For he'd many miles to trot that night
Before he reached his den O!

The first place he came to was a farmer's yard,
Where the ducks and the geese declared it hard
That their nerves should be shaken and their rest so marred
By a visit from Mr. Fox O!
    Fox O! Fox O!
That their nerves should be shaken and their rest so marred
By a visit from Mr. Fox O!

He took the grey goose by the neck,
And swung him right across his back;
The grey goose cried out, Quack, quack, quack,
With his legs hanging dangling down O!
    Down O! Down O!
The grey goose cried out, Quack, quack, quack,
With his legs hanging dangling down O!

Old Mother Slipper Slopper jumped out of bed,
And out of the window she popped her head:
Oh! John, John, John, the grey goose is gone,
And the fox is off to his den O!
　　Den O! Den O!
Oh! John, John, John, the grey goose is gone,
And the fox is off to his den O!

John ran up to the top of the hill,
And blew his whistle loud and shrill;
Said the fox, That is very pretty music; still —
I'd rather be in my den O!
　　Den O! Den O!
Said the fox, That is very pretty music; still —
I'd rather be in my den O!

The fox went back to his hungry den,
And his dear little foxes, eight, nine, ten;
Quoth they, Good daddy, you must go there again,
If you bring such good cheer from the farm O!
　　Farm O! Farm O!
Quoth they, Good daddy, you must go there again,
If you bring such good cheer from the farm O!

The fox and his wife, without any strife,
Said they never ate a better goose in all their life;
They did very well without fork or knife,
And the little ones picked the bones O!
　　Bones O! Bones O!
They did very well without fork or knife,
And the little ones picked the bones O!

The Little Woman and the Pedlar

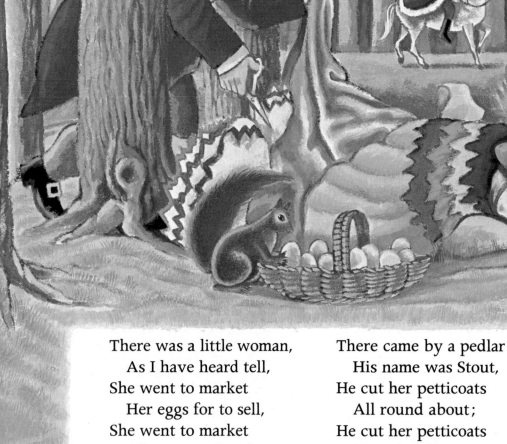

There was a little woman,
  As I have heard tell,
She went to market
  Her eggs for to sell,
She went to market
  All on a market day,
And she fell asleep
  On the King's highway.

There came by a pedlar
  His name was Stout,
He cut her petticoats
  All round about;
He cut her petticoats
  Up to her knees,
Which made the poor woman
  To shiver and sneeze.

When the little woman
    Began to awake,
She began to shiver,
    And she began to shake;
She began to shake,
    And she began to cry,
Goodness mercy on me,
    This is none of I!

If it be not I,
    As I suppose it be,
I have a little dog at home,
    And he knows me;
If it be I,
    He'll wag his little tail,
And if it be not I,
    He'll loudly bark and wail.

Home went the little woman,
    All in the dark,
Up jumped the little dog,
    And he began to bark,
He began to bark,
    And she began to cry,
Goodness mercy on me,
    I see I be not I!

Playtime

I'm the king of the castle,
Get down you dirty rascal.

Finders keepers,
Losers weepers.

Lucy Locket lost her pocket,
Kitty Fisher found it;
Not a penny was there in it,
Only ribbon round it.

Tell tale tit,
Your tongue shall be split
And all the little puppy dogs,
Shall have a little bit!

Here am I,
  Little Jumping Joan;
When nobody's with me
  I'm all alone.

I'll sing you a song,
Nine verses long,
  For a pin;
Three and three are six,
And three are nine;
You are a fool,
  And the pin is mine.

The Toy Cupboard

Little John Jiggy Jag,
He rode a penny nag,
  And went to Wigan to woo:
When he came to a beck,
He fell and broke his neck,
  Johnny, how dost thou now?

I made him a hat
Of my coat lap,
  And stockings of pearly blue;
A hat and a feather,
To keep out cold weather,
  So, Johnny, how dost thou now?

I had a little moppet,
I kept it in my pocket
And fed it on corn and hay;
There came a proud beggar
And said he would wed her,
And stole my little moppet away.

Hushy baby, my doll, I pray you don't cry,
And I'll give you some bread and some milk by and by;
Or, perhaps you like custard, or may be a tart,
Then to either you're welcome, with all my whole heart.

Jerry Hall,
He is so small,
A rat could eat him,
Hat and all.

Cobbler, cobbler, mend my shoe,
Get it done by half past two;
Stitch it up, and stitch it down,
And I will give you half a crown

My maid Mary,
She minds the dairy,
While I go a-hoeing and mowing
each morn;
Merrily runs the reel,
And the little spinning wheel,
Whilst I am singing and mowing
my corn.

Wash the dishes, wipe the dishes,
Ring the bell for tea;
Three good wishes, three good
kisses,
I will give to thee.

Work and Play

There was a jolly miller once,
   Lived on the river Dee;
He worked and sang from morn till night,
   No lark so blithe as he.
And this the burden of his song
   For ever used to be,
I care for nobody – no! not I,
   If nobody cares for me.

Meadowsweet,
And thistledown,
Up the hill,
And tumble down.

Can you wash your father's shirt,
   Can you wash it clean?
Can you wash your father's shirt
   And bleach it on the green?
Yes, I can wash my father's shirt,
   And I can wash it clean.
I can wash my father's shirt
   And send it to the Queen.

See-saw, Margery Daw,
Jacky shall have a new master;
Jacky shall have but a penny a day,
Because he can't work any faster.

Strange folk

Goosey, goosey gander,
   Whither shall I wander?
Upstairs and downstairs
   And in my lady's chamber.
There I met an old man
   Who would not say his prayers,
I took him by the left leg
   And threw him down the stairs.

There was a crooked man
   And he walked a crooked mile;
He found a crooked sixpence
   Against a crooked stile;
He bought a crooked cat
   Which caught a crooked mouse,
And they all lived together
   In a little crooked house.

Peter, Peter, pumpkin eater,
Had a wife and couldn't keep her;
He put her in a pumpkin shell
And there he kept her very well.

Peter, Peter, pumpkin eater,
Had another, and didn't love her;
Peter learned to read and spell,
And then he loved her very well.

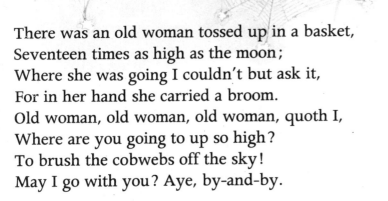

Mrs. Mason bought a basin,
Mrs. Tyson said, What a nice 'un,
What did it cost? said Mrs. Frost,
Half a crown, said Mrs. Brown,
Did it indeed, said Mrs. Reed,
It did for certain, said Mrs. Burton.
Then Mrs. Nix up to her tricks
Threw the basin on the bricks.

There was an old woman tossed up in a basket,
Seventeen times as high as the moon;
Where she was going I couldn't but ask it,
For in her hand she carried a broom.
Old woman, old woman, old woman, quoth I,
Where are you going to up so high?
To brush the cobwebs off the sky!
May I go with you? Aye, by-and-by.

Doctor Foster went to Gloucester
In a shower of rain;
He stepped in a puddle,
Right up to his middle,
And never went there again.

Soldier, Soldier

Oh, soldier, soldier, will you marry me,
  With your musket, fife, and drum?
Oh no, pretty maid, I cannot marry you,
  For I have no coat to put on.

Then away she went
  To her grandfather's chest,
And bought him one of the very very best,
  And the soldier put it on.

Oh, soldier, soldier, will you marry me,
  With your musket, fife, and drum?
Oh no, pretty maid, I cannot marry you,
  For I have no socks to put on.

Then away she went
  To her grandfather's chest,
And bought him a pair of the very very best,
  And the soldier put them on.

Oh, soldier, soldier, will you marry me,
  With your musket, fife, and drum?
Oh no, pretty maid, I cannot marry you,
  For I have no shoes to put on.

Then away she went
  To her grandfather's chest,
And bought him a pair of the very very best,
  And the soldier put them on.

Oh, soldier, soldier, will you marry me,
　With your musket, fife, and drum?
Oh no, pretty maid, I cannot marry you,
　For I have no hat to put on.

Then away she went
　To her grandfather's chest,
And bought him one of the very very best,
　And the soldier put it on.

Oh, soldier, soldier, will you marry me,
　With your musket fife, and drum?
Oh no, pretty maid, I cannot marry you,
　For I have a wife at home.

Fights and fisticuffs

The lion and the unicorn
    Were fighting for the crown;
The lion beat the unicorn
    All around the town.

Some gave them white bread,
    And some gave them brown;
Some gave them plum cake
    And drummed them out of town.

Tweedledum and Tweedledee
    Agreed to have a battle,
For Tweedledum said Tweedledee
    Had spoiled his nice new rattle.
Just then flew by a monstrous crow
    As big as a tar-barrel,
Which frightened both the heroes so,
    They quite forgot their quarrel.

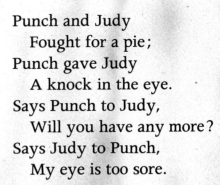

Punch and Judy
   Fought for a pie;
Punch gave Judy
   A knock in the eye.
Says Punch to Judy,
   Will you have any more?
Says Judy to Punch,
   My eye is too sore.

Oh, the grand old Duke of York,
He had ten thousand men;
He marched them up
To the top of the hill,
And he marched them down again.

And when they were up,
They were up,
And when they were down, they were down.
And when they were only half-way up,
They were neither up nor down.

Kings and Queens

Hector Protector was dressed all in green;
Hector Protector was sent to the Queen.
 The Queen did not like him,
 No more did the King;
So Hector Protector was sent back again.

Old King Cole
 Was a merry old soul,
And a merry old soul was he;
 He called for his pipe,
 And he called for his bowl,
And he called for his fiddlers three.

Every fiddler he had a fiddle,
And a very fine fiddle had he;
 Oh, there's none so rare
 As can compare
With King Cole and his fiddlers
 three.

The Queen of Hearts
She made some tarts,
All on a summer's day;
The Knave of Hearts
He stole those tarts,
And took them clean away.

The King of Hearts
Called for the tarts,
And beat the knave full sore;
The Knave of Hearts
Brought back the tarts,
And vowed he'd steal no more.

I had a little nut tree,
Nothing would it bear
But a silver nutmeg
And a golden pear;
The king of Spain's daughter
Came to visit me,
And all for the sake
Of my little nut tree.
I skipped over water,
I danced over sea,
And all the birds in the air
Couldn't catch me.

Lavender's blue, diddle, diddle,
Lavender's green;
When I am king, diddle, diddle,
You shall be queen.

Tall Stories

Little King Pippin
   He built a fine hall,
Pie-crust and pastry-crust
   That was the wall;
The windows were made
   Of black pudding and white,
And slated with pancakes,
   You ne'er saw the like.

Oh, dear, what can the matter be?
Two old women got up in an apple-tree;
One came down,
And the other stayed till Saturday.

Terence McDiddler,
    The three-stringed fiddler,
Can charm, if you please,
    The fish from the seas.

What's the news of the day,
Good neighbour, I pray?
They say the balloon
Is gone up to the moon.

Bow-wow
says the dog

I had a dog
   Whose name was Buff,
I sent him for
   A bag of snuff;
He broke the bag
   And spilled the stuff,
And that was all
   My penny's worth.

Bow-wow, says the dog,
Mew, mew, says the cat,
Grunt, grunt, goes the hog,
And squeak goes the rat.
Tu-whu, says the owl,
Caw, caw, says the crow,
Quack, quack, says the duck,
And what cuckoos say you know.

I had a dog and his name was Dandy,
His tail was long and his legs were bandy,
His eyes were brown and his coat was sandy,
The best in the world was my dog Dandy.

90

Oh where, oh where has my little dog gone?
   Oh where, oh where can he be?
With his ears cut short and his tail cut long,
   Oh where, oh where is he?

Hark, hark,
  The dogs do bark,
The beggars are coming to town;
  Some in rags,
  And some in jags,
And one in a velvet gown.

My Mother Said

My mother said
That I never should
Play with the gipsies
In the wood;
If I did she would say,
Naughty girl to disobey.
Your hair shan't curl,
Your shoes shan't shine,
You naughty girl
You shan't be mine.
My father said
That if I did
He'd bang my head
With the teapot lid.

The wood was dark
The grass was green,
Up comes Sally
With a tambourine;
Alpaca frock,
New scarf-shawl,
White straw bonnet
And a pink parasol.
I went to the river—
No ship to get across,
I paid ten shillings
For an old blind horse;
I up on his back
And off in a crack,
Sally tell my mother
I shall never come back.

All the fun of the fair

BANBURY FAIR

Smiling girls, rosy boys,
Come and buy my little toys;
Monkeys made of gingerbread,
And sugar horses painted red.

As I was going to Banbury,
  Upon a summer's day,
My dame had butter, eggs, and fruit,
  And I had corn and hay.
Joe drove the ox, and Tom the swine,
  Dick took the foal and mare;
I sold them all, then home to dine,
  From famous Banbury fair.

94

Gee up, Neddy, to the fair,
What shall I buy when I get there?
A ha'penny apple, a penny pear.
Gee-up, Neddy, to the fair.

Hot cross buns! Hot cross buns!
One a penny, two a penny,
Hot cross buns!
If your daughters do not like them
Give them to your sons;
One a penny, two a penny,
Hot cross buns.

Join hands!

Poor Mary lies a-weeping, a-weeping, a-weeping,
Poor Mary lies a-weeping, on a bright summer's day!

Oh, why is she a-weeping, a-weeping, a-weeping?
Oh, why is she a-weeping, on a bright summer's day?

She's weeping for her true love, her true love, her true love,
She's weeping for her true love, on a bright summer's day.

On the carpet she must kneel,
Till the grass grows in the field,
Stand up now, upon your feet,
Choose the one you love so sweet!

Now you're married we wish you joy,
First the girl, and then the boy.
Kiss her once, kiss her twice,
Kiss her three times over!

Ring-a-ring o'roses,
A pocket full of posies,
    A-tishoo! A-tishoo!
We all fall down.

The cows are in the meadow
Lying fast asleep,
    A-tishoo! A-tishoo!
We all get up again.

Oh Dear, what can the Matter be?

Oh, dear, what can the matter be?
Dear, dear, what can the matter be?
Oh, dear, what can the matter be?
Johnny's so long at the fair.

He promised he'd buy me a fairing should please me,
And then for a kiss, oh! he vowed he would tease me,
He promised he'd bring me a bunch of blue ribbons
To tie up my bonny brown hair.

Oh, dear, what can the matter be?
Dear, dear, what can the matter be?
Oh, dear, what can the matter be?
Johnny's so long at the fair.

He promised he'd bring me a basket of posies,
A garland of lilies, a garland of roses,
A little straw hat, to set off the blue ribbons
That tie up my bonny brown hair.

Oh, dear, what can the matter be?
Dear, dear, what can the matter be?
Oh, dear, what can the matter be?
Johnny's so long at the fair.

Little love ditties

Curly locks, Curly locks,
    Wilt thou be mine?
Thou shalt not wash dishes
    Nor yet feed the swine;
But sit on a cushion
    And sew a fine seam,
And feed upon strawberries,
    Sugar and cream.

What are little boys made of, made of?
What are little boys made of?
    Frogs and snails
    And puppy-dogs' tails,
That's what little boys are made of.

What are little girls made of, made of?
What are little girls made of?
    Sugar and spice
    And all things nice,
That's what little girls are made of.

One I love,
Two I love,
Three I love, I say,
Four I love with all my heart,
Five I cast away;
Six he loves me,
Seven he don't,
Eight we're lovers both;
Nine he comes,
Ten he tarries,
Eleven he courts,
Twelve he marries.

She loves me,
She loves me not,
She loves me,
She loves me not,
She loves me!

He loves me,
He don't,
He'll have me,
He won't,
He would
If he could,
But he can't,
So he don't.

Roses are red,
Violets are blue,
Sugar is sweet
And so are you.

Are we nearly there?

Three wise men of Gotham
Went to sea in a bowl;
If the bowl had been stronger,
My story would have been longer.

How many miles to Babylon?
Three-score and ten.
Can I get there by candle-light?
Yes, and back again.
If your heels are nimble and light,
You may get there by candle-light.

See-saw, sacradown,
Which is the way to London town?
One foot up and the other foot down,
That is the way to London town.

The man in the moon
Came down too soon,
And asked his way to Norwich;
He went by the south,
And burned his mouth
With supping cold plum porridge.

Where are you going to, my pretty maid?

Where are you going to, my pretty maid?
I'm going a-milking, sir, she said,
Sir, she said, sir, she said,
I'm going a-milking, sir, she said.

May I go with you, my pretty maid?
You're kindly welcome, sir, she said,
Sir, she said, sir, she said,
You're kindly welcome, sir, she said.

Say, will you marry me, my pretty maid?
Yes, if you please, kind sir, she said,
Sir, she said, sir, she said,
Yes, if you please, kind sir, she said.

What is your father, my pretty maid?
My father's a farmer, sir, she said,
Sir, she said, sir, she said,
My father's a farmer, sir, she said.

What is your fortune, my pretty maid?
My face is my fortune, sir, she said,
Sir, she said, sir, she said,
My face is my fortune, sir, she said.

Then I can't marry you, my pretty maid.
Nobody asked you, sir, she said,
Sir, she said, sir, she said,
Nobody asked you, sir, she said.

Bobby Shaftoe

Bobby Shaftoe's gone to sea,
Silver buckles at his knee;
He'll come back and marry me,
    Bonny Bobby Shaftoe.

Bobby Shaftoe's bright and fair,
Combing down his yellow hair,
He's my ain for evermair,
    Bonny Bobby Shaftoe.

Bobby Shaftoe's tall and slim,
He's always dressed so neat and trim,
The ladies they all keek at him,
   Bonny Bobby Shaftoe.

Bobby Shaftoe's getten a bairn
For to dandle in his arm;
In his arm and on his knee,
   Bobby Shaftoe loves me.

Over land and sea

My mother sent me for some water,
For some water from the sea,
My foot slipped, and in I tumbled,
Three jolly sailors came to me:
One said he'd buy me silks and satins,
One said he'd buy me a guinea gold ring,
One said he'd buy me a silver cradle
For to rock my baby in.

If all the seas were one sea,
   What a great sea that would be!
If all the trees were one tree,
   What a great tree that would be!
And if all the axes were one axe,
   What a great axe that would be!
And if all the men were one man,
   What a great man that would be!
And if the great man took the great axe,
   And cut down the great tree,
And let it fall into the great sea,
   What a splish-splash that would be!

If all the world was paper,
And all the sea was ink,
If all the trees were bread and cheese,
What should we have to drink?

Over the water and over the lea,
And over the water to Charlie.
I'll have none of your nasty beef,
Nor I'll have none of your barley,
But I'll have some of your very best flour
To make a white cake for my Charlie.

Little Tee Wee,
He went to sea
In an open boat:
And while afloat
The little boat bended,
And my story's ended.

109

Here we go round the Mulberry Bush

Here we go round the mulberry bush,
The mulberry bush, the mulberry bush,
Here we go round the mulberry bush,
On a cold and frosty morning.

This is the way we wash our hands,
Wash our hands, wash our hands,
This is the way we wash our hands,
On a cold and frosty morning.

This is the way we wash our clothes,
Wash our clothes, wash our clothes,
This is the way we wash our clothes,
On a cold and frosty morning.

This is the way we go to school,
Go to school, go to school,
This is the way we go to school,
On a cold and frosty morning.

This is the way we come out of school,
Come out of school, come out of school,
This is the way we come out of school,
On a cold and frosty morning.

Winter songs

The north wind doth blow,
And we shall have snow,
And what will poor Robin do then?
    Poor thing.
He'll sit in a barn,
And keep himself warm,
And hide his head under his wing,
    Poor thing.

Button to chin
When October comes in.
Cast not a clout
Till May be out.

Cuckoo, cuckoo, cherry tree,
Catch a bird, and give it me;
Let the tree be high or low,
Let it hail or rain or snow.

Snow, snow faster,
Ally-ally-blaster;
The old woman's plucking her geese,
Selling the feathers a penny a piece.

Jingle, bells! jingle, bells!
Jingle all the way:
Oh, what fun it is to ride
In a one-horse open sleigh.

Christmas time

Little Jack Horner
Sat in the corner,
Eating a Christmas pie;
He put in his thumb,
And pulled out a plum,
And said, What a good boy am I!

God bless the master of this hou
And its good mistress too,
And all the little children
That round the table go;
And all your kin and kinsmen,
That dwell both far and near;
We wish you a merry Christmas
And a happy New Year.

Merry are the bells, and merry would they ring,
Merry was myself, and merry could I sing;
With a merry ding-dong, happy, gay, and free,
And a merry sing-song, happy let us be.

Christmas is coming,
    The geese are getting fat,
Please put a penny
    In the old man's hat.
If you haven't got a penny,
    A ha'penny will do;
If you haven't got a ha'penny,
    Then God bless you!

Hush Little Baby

Hush, little baby, don't say a word,
Papa's going to buy you a mocking bird.

If the mocking bird won't sing,
Papa's going to buy you a diamond ring.

If the diamond ring turns to brass,
Papa's going to buy you a looking-glass.

If the looking-glass gets broke,
Papa's going to buy you a billy-goat.

If that billy-goat runs away,
Papa's going to buy you another today.

Time for bed . . .

Boys and girls come out to play,
The moon doth shine as bright as day.
Leave your supper and leave your sleep,
And join your playfellows in the street.
Come with a whoop and come with a call,
Come with a good will or not at all.
Up the ladder and down the wall,
A half-penny loaf will serve us all;
You find milk, and I'll find flour,
And we'll have a pudding in half an hour.

Wee Willie Winkie runs through the town,
Upstairs and downstairs in his night-gown,
Rapping at the window, crying through the lock,
Are all the children in their beds, for now it's eight o'clock?

Jack be nimble,
Jack be quick,
Jack jump over
The candlestick.

Twinkle, twinkle, little star,
How I wonder what you are!
Up above the world so high,
Like a diamond in the sky.

119

Put out the light...

Come, let's to bed,
Says Sleepy-head;
Tarry a while, says Slow;
Put on the pot,
Says Greedy-gut,
We'll sup before we go.

Rock-a-bye, baby,
    Thy cradle is green,
Father's a nobleman,
    Mother's a queen;
And Betty's a lady,
    And wears a gold ring;
And Johnny's a drummer,
    And drums for the king.

Go to bed first,
A golden purse;
Go to bed second,
A golden pheasant;
Go to bed third,
A golden bird.

Down with the lambs,
Up with the lark,
Run to bed children
Before it gets dark.

Good night, God bless you,
Go to bed and undress you.

Good night, sweet repose,
Half the bed and all the clothes.

Goodnight!

I see the moon,
   And the moon sees me;
God bless the moon,
   And God bless me.

Index of titles and first lines

Good night